INSPIRATIONS

FOR THE SPIRITUALLY AWARE PARENT

BY CHRISTINA FLETCHER

Reactions to

Inspirations for the Spiritually Aware Parent

I'm a mother of two little ones. Many if not all of your messages have really spoke to my heart. I want to help my children blossom and have a close connection with God. Thank you for your insights and ideas to parent lovingly.- Tiffany

I love the new insight I gain by reading many of your passages. In this fast paced world we live in its nice to be reminded that there's a different approach we can take with our children. So they to can embrace others with love & kindness. - Kelli

You are totally insightful and it is refreshing to read your posts. I have 3 bebes and love your wisdom and approach to parenting as I am on my journey! Love & light!- Shell

Introduction

I am so happy to be able to bring this book to you and share the ever-growing experience of Spiritually Aware Parenting.

This book contains a selection of the passages I wrote through 2012 for my Facebook Page Spiritually Aware Parenting and what an exciting journey this year has been.

When I started my nightly practice of writing words of inspiration for my Facebook page, based on what I was observing, learning, and tapping into each day, I never expected to still be typing away after all this time. I also never expected to receive such wonderful support, questions, and encouragement as I have with my beautiful Facebook community. For so long social networking was about sharing photos and jokes or talking about problems, but now, as I head into my third year with SAP, it has become a place of co-creation, love and inspiration not just for me, but for parents all over the world.

I choke that back a bit, really as it seems presumptuous or impossible. I'm in such awe of it, but now with almost 3500 members these passages have transcended gender, race, and spiritual dogma, and so far, it has been a page full of love and understanding for who we all are at our core. For that I am eternally grateful.

Within these pages you will find moments of relief, reminders of how to go within, to trust your inner voice. There are passages to tap into our children as who they are at their core, perspective shifters to see them anew, there are pointers on understanding negative emotion in ourselves and in our children, and shout outs to remember to play and have fun.

Perhaps the last is the most important. Life is about fun. It is the greatest game and it needs to have less stress applied to it. These passages are my connection point, they are for fun and my interaction with the people in my online community, as we co-create together, is one of my greatest joys.

So here's to all of you, parents everywhere. May this book inspire, uplift and shift perspective from a bad day getting worse, but may it also bring a smile to your face sometimes. Smiling is one of the best things we can do in this world and if my words can help in anyway, that is my greatest joy and it fills me with wonder, awe and appreciation.

Be well, happy and thrive.

Dedication

To my husband, Jeff,

the perfect partner in life, who lights up each day with just a look in his eyes, who is the perfect cure for an off day and who makes good days all the better. Thanks for being a sounding board to my perspective shifting.

To our children, Abi, Gia, and Freddie.

You are perfect and I am so proud of everything you are. Thank you for helping me learn and grow and for bringing such wonderful joy into each day, with loads of laughter and overwhelming love. Thank you for choosing us, for being your wonderful selves and for sharing this experience.

To the Spiritually Aware Parenting community.

You made this book, for without your support these words would have gone unwritten and faded as past thoughts. Thank you.

Lastly, to my Source, God, inner voice,

Without you, the words would not be found, the thoughts would not be thought, and I would not have the golden thread so often dangled in front of me to help me find my own connection. I appreciate it with all of my being.

Savour the relief when you appreciate the little things.

Appreciate the small things you see your children do... or not do.

Appreciate their excitement, and their intense feelings that are focused entirely in the moment.

Appreciate their vantage point, their perspective, which will change constantly as they grow.

Savour your children, in their off and on moments,

for therein lies the happy parent.

To consciously create a day doesn't mean we plan each second and then be surprised when it doesn't transpire.

Rather by focusing on the positive aspects of life and by consciously focusing on the elements that feel good, we radiate at a feeling space that will attract more of the same.

Scientifically, we also become more broadminded, being able to see solutions rather than problems.

Therefore, choose to feel good.

When someone we love and care for is going through an off time, it's easy to slip into worry, concern and stress about them.

In doing so we think we're helping, but in fact we're doing two things that can't offer support. First we risk losing our own connection if we spend too long staring at the problem and second by seeing the offness in them we take a picture of it and use it as the reference point of who they are, thereby giving them no room to grow and change from the experience.

The best help we can offer is to focus on the truest part of them, and look only at the best, acknowledging the problem, but focused on the soul-ution.

We shouldn't be too quick to teach our children to rationalize their dreams

and we should try to not use logic to create our future plans.

For it is in the dreaming,

the imagining,

the aspiring,

that the spark of life flows forth, whether the specifics transpire or not.

It is the spark of the desire that create similar experiences.

Therefore, dream big and savour the dream itself, not just the having of the result.

*Our children see us as Who We Really Are
and often they stand there, trying to call us
back to ourselves.*

*When we are stressed and frantic, they
sensed our lack of joy and they ask to play, as
that's what they know we need.*

*What, in our disconnection, we think is ill-
timed or that we're too busy, we feel they get
pushy and try to distract them, in turn they
seem to ask to play more.*

*When we turn to them, and accept their
invitation, distracting ourselves with playing
and joy-full moments, than within a short
period of time, their anxiety will be gone and
our to-do list, which seemed so stressful, will
suddenly be easier or seem less important
than we thought it was,*

as in connection all things flow downstream.

We can be the balance in our home.

When our children are over-excited or feeling un-centered we can come in as the calmer, grounded energy, by breathing deep, talking slower and changing the feeling space we walk in.

If others are feeling sad and discouraged, we can be the ones who find the inner fire, sparking life and being love, joy and laughter.

When we feel something we don't like in our house, or in places we go, it doesn't have to rub us the wrong way, nor do we have to give into it, rather we can breathe deep, connect to our inner re-Sources

and shift the energy space ourselves.

Sometimes days just don't go as planned,

no matter how much we try to force things to go as we think is best.

When this is the situation it is only by letting go of the plan,

by taking a step back,

releasing what we think *is best,*

and choosing to feel better in the now,

that we can relax and see what the universal powers have in mind instead.

We may not accomplish what we had planned, but we will have created a space to feel better in

and that always creates better tomorrows.

A child has the unique gift to shift feeling spaces quickly.

They want to feel good and they don't feel the social pressure to ride a mood through its course before feeling better.

It is a wonderful thing to watch a child hunt around for the better feeling option and once they find it, or are offered it, jump head first into following it.

When we offer awareness to children,

helping them look for better feeling options from an early age, it sets the foundation as one where feeling better is a choice, and when we seize the moment and choose to focus on something that brings relief, rather than feeling we have to stew in a pot of pain, we can shift perspectives quickly without feeling like we should have stewed longer first!

Although, as pure positive spirits, children feel most themselves when they are feeling happy, having fun and full of joy sometimes laughter and hysteria can be a sign of disconnection.

When our children are feeling overwhelmed, unfocused, and spinning from over excitement or stimulation, even too much computer games or fast paced TV, there is a disconnected level of play that just doesn't feel right.

As parents if we see our children having fun, it can feel off to stop them from playing, so rather it can be a process of shifting focus, creating an activity that has a calming effect and slowing down the energy like a train pulling into a station.

Then a child can connect easily and find the grounded space within to truly enjoy life once again.

Our children have wants and desires too and the flow of universal wellbeing is flooding towards them trying to take care of them, just as it does for all of us.

Often, as parents, we are so eager to help our children achieve their dreams that we end up working upstream, struggling, to make them happen, even if it stresses us out.

When we remember that it's up to their connection to let it flow in, as well as our own, we can relax and simply do our best.

We can remind them that everything is created through feeling good and being happy in our now. There is no point in struggling, for when we do we build up a dam to the good stuff flowing in, and when our children are connected, even if we aren't, it's amazing how fast their desires are met, without life getting too hairy for any of us.

Say Yes!

It's easy to get into the habit of constantly saying no.

We say no to our children, to opportunities, to people we meet. We come up with excuses why we can't do something, can't go somewhere, can't play.

However, when we say yes whenever we find ourselves looking for an excuse to say no, when we accept invitations to take part in life, we open up to opportunities to grow, expand, learn and laugh.

Sure, there are lots of things that we need to say no to, those that are really impossible, but when we can't find concrete reasons, we should always try a Yes, and open up the door to new worlds.

Once our children are a little older,

we don't need to tell them what not to do or what to do. We don't need to tell our children what to eat, say, or be.

Rather, it is a more joyful and fulfilling path to offer our children WHY we think they should or shouldn't do something, WHY it's a good idea to eat something, what we would say in situations, and then trust them to BE themselves.

Telling our children things is simply an act of pushing against life, trying to control the uncontrollable, and forgetting to see them as themselves.

Explaining things to them is expanding their perspective, offering them insight and helping them form their own opinions.

We create the space we feel every day.

Oh yes, sometimes things happen that can throw us into turmoil, but the everyday, doing every day sort of things, we choose to react to things, or act on things, or just stop and be about things.

That's a powerful thing, as we often get caught up in the idea that we are a victim to our circumstance.

In fact, we can walk away from things that make us mad, we can breathe our way through stress, we can distract from frustration.

When we are aware of how we feel we can face it and then shift from it, being honest in the process.

The more we feel how we choose, the more that builds up steam, and in doing so the more life flows in on that feeling space.

Children feel everything to the core of their being.

Therefore when good things are coming their way, they are filled to the brim with the expectation of it, when they are having fun, their cup overflows!

On the opposite side of the coin, when they are disconnected, when shopping days, or headaches are causing pain and frustration, they see no light and they are overwhelmed by the feeling of offness.

When we offer them relief by shining some light on the situation, shifting attention to other things that make them feel better, we offer them tools for the future, whereas if we get frustrated by their frustration, we are simply compounding the situation.

Look for the things going well.

Often as parents we want to help and create the better feeling options for ourselves and our children, when really, when we look around, things are going quite well without our interference.

Be ready to sit back and enjoy the wellbeing that flows for all of us.

There will always be off days, but when we enjoy the on and appreciate the flow, not only will we be able to feel the off days better, we will also create the space for the flow to keep flooding our lives.

Our children watch us and feel through their higher senses how we work each day.

They feel our stress, our distraction and our connection.

By doing simple things like sitting quietly for a few minutes to get grounded and focused, or by stopping mid-way in a stressful situation to find an inner peace, we offer the tools of happier living to our children.

We don't have to get it right all the time. Our children will feel the difference between our connected moments and our disconnected ones, and in feeling it they will see our inner work and try it out for themselves in the future.

"To do" lists, "Should do "lists and "have to get to that" impulses so often let us miss the magic moments of our children's childhoods.

We speed past things, asking our children to rush with us while they are wiser to realize the living is in the appreciation of every flower, insect and wrinkle of a toy's blanket.

We are so lucky to have our connected ones beside us, for they understand things we have forgotten and when we connect with them, often our bodies and spirits tingle with the delight of being true to our deepest core.

Taking the simple route, the one with the least struggle, is usually the one which opens up to a new perspective and opportunity.

Often we can bang about problems and get so use to having stress in our lives that even if the problem gets solved we are quick to jump to the next.

By letting go of problems, reaching for the easiest solution, and then allowing wellbeing to flow through, we will feel lighter and stay connected to ourselves,

letting universal powers take on at least half the load.

We can learn a lot by looking out for indicators that show us that we're keeping aligned to everything we really are.

When we are connected most of the time things flow in a general direction of wellbeing.

Yes, we feel great when we're connected, but also we skip out on traffic, we catch the bus on time, and we get the last sale item before they sell out. We can call these small bonuses just luck, or we can see them, and appreciate them, as signs we're doing generally alright.

On the same token, when everything is difficult and we can't even wash as dish without it even breaking,

then it's time to go within, catch up with ourselves and work ourselves back to connection.

Source is always working with us and will get our attention in whatever way will make us take notice.

It never feels good to get mad or to hold onto anger.

It never makes us feel happy or ourselves to try to gain control over others or try to MAKE others understand.

When things don't feel good within the deepest core of ourselves, then it is an indicator that it's not aligned to Who We Really Are

If it's not aligned it can never work out well.

Therefore, even though it doesn't make any logical or social sense, getting mad or trying to gain control of our children isn't aligned to who we or our children really are.

Rather by seeing them as the true spiritual beings we all are, we can connect to our source, connect with them and work together for the peaceful solutions.

Breathe, focus on things that make you feel better and relax.

We don't need to know how the story ends, or the hidden purpose of why it happens the way it does.

We don't need to torment ourselves with how to be the "perfect" parent, or how to raise the "perfect" child.

You are perfectly You.

They are Perfectly themselves.

Without knowing it you are creating your perfect story, relax, reach for joy

and let it all in.

When a child is fussy or acting unlike themselves then often the simple act of playing with them can call them back to themselves.

It's so easy to fall back into the habit of saying no or getting stressed and upset, when really they are trying to stop life from being confusing and slow it down so they can get connected.

When we ourselves get connected we can feel our way to what our children are crying out for, and often, unless they are sick or tired, a focused game of some sort will call them back.

Play and having fun can connect all of us.

Life is like swimming, when we struggle against it and fear it, we begin to sink, raising more fear and anxiety.

However, when we allow ourselves to float, when we relax our bodies letting the water lift us up and carry us, it's easy.

Life is meant to be easy, as there is so much universal power that carries us and supports us.

There is nothing to struggle against, even if things in our lives would try to convince us of otherwise.

We simply need to float... and go with the flow.

We all like to be seen as the best aspects of ourselves.

We all like to be listened to, appreciated and even more so forgiven when we make mistakes.

We all like our best stories told and our worst forgotten.

Our children feel the same.

By treating our children the same way we wish to be treated, we not only provide them an example of the best tool in life, but we offer them the chance to be their authentic selves.

It is time we gave children a break from seeing them as "children" and us as "adults". We are all spiritual beings playing together and by seeing each other as equal we create a place where everyone can express themselves as Who They Really Are.

Life is a progression of experiences, each building upon each other.

We don't grow up, we simply live.

An infant experiences life on one scale which then builds to the toddler stage, defining and redefining their perspective, which then builds to the next stage.

This building upon experiences, defining our opinions and perspectives, shaping what we like and what we dislike, creating ourselves and tapping into everything we really are, goes on for the rest of our lives.

We are a work in progress, and in reminding ourselves of the journey, rather than the destination, we can see life as the wonderful adventure our children see it as,

throw caution to the wind, and live.

We have to trust our children's journey just as we do our own.

Although things may feel complicated at any given moment, it is by trusting in wellbeing and in the joyful moment to joyful moment living process that we can learn to let go of the details that may not always make sense.

Sometimes it feels our children have wound themselves up too intensely and we can worry about the results.

However, when we relax, look for each better feeling moment, and reassure them of the wellness that flows around all of us, then we will always look back at those rough times and see that it was the perfect catalyst for the things that came after.

It never matters how justified we feel for complaining or reacting negatively to something, and throwing in guilt afterwards never helps either.

We achieve nothing from a negative space, except growth.

Sometimes we are simply disconnected and it's time to connect again.

Our children know when we're disconnected, so we might as well admit it.

Let the day go, find peace somehow, even though distraction, breathe and relax.

Tomorrow is another day and if we take the time to connect first and act after, everything will appear in a different perspective.

After all, everything's perfect, even in our growth.

It takes only one feeling better thought to shift the run of an off day.

Sometimes, when we are feeling frustrated or overwhelmed we can bang about the idea of feeling better, but it can seem like nothing helps.

It feels like a spiral, that just continues spiralling

. It helps to know that one thought can make that shift. It just takes trying on different ones to find the right fit.

Therefore, we can appreciate, we can visualize, we can dream, we can play.

We don't need to commit to how we feel at the moment, only commit to finding the path to feeling better.

Our children are each individual miracle workers.

When we take a moment to see them work their magic it can fill us with awe on how they make the world such a better place.

So often we get caught up in trying to tell them how to be, that we forget...

they already know.

Often when we have things that we have to do, we push against our children's needs, asking them to wait until we're done doing what we feel is urgent.

When we relax in that urgency and are honest with them, allowing them to help or feel like they are part of the process rather than feeling they are in the way, then we can regain balance and the urgency relaxes, allowing the things that need to get done flow through us rather than push us to being disconnected from ourselves.

A day offers up so many opportunities to stop and get connected to our true selves, it's just reminding ourselves to find them.

Nursing our babies, washing dishes, peeling potatoes, even traffic all provide the space to stop and think things that feel good, or just drop into a feeling good space, if we just let them.

So often we go through these actions and let our minds chatter away negatively or create to do lists and stress.

But when we start to feel our mouths turn into a soft smile and feel the release of stress through connection, than we know that we have used our time wisely taking any old moment as a spiritual space in time.

A parent's day can often be filled with moments of frustration or stress.

However, when we act upon those moments we perpetuate them, creating more of the same.

When we take a step back, and see them as the indicators of disconnection they really are, we can shift focus, appreciating what we have or focusing on things that make us feel better.

When we take the effort to feel better first and act after,

we readjust of antenna to pick up a clearer reception to Who We Really Are.

No matter how many times we tell our children how wonderful they are, how special they are, how beautiful they are, it is only when we see them as such, that they will truly believe us.

Therefore, take time to watch your children each day.

Appreciate who they are as they play, cherish them as they walk outside, marvel at them when they laugh, love them as they speak about their day.

When we take the time to appreciate Who our Children Are, we are telling them how amazing they are, without the need of words, and offering them the basement for

true self esteem.

We can always find the signs that wellbeing is flowing.

Little things that go well happen all the time, it's just that we have learnt to take them for granted or consider them simply "good luck".

There is no such thing as luck, it is simply alignment to the wellbeing that flows and the Source from where that wellbeing flows from. Usually that alignment happens when we let go of trying to control the situation, and that's why it's in the little things where it first appears.

We have all lost something and not found it until we've stopped looking for it! Look for the little things that go well and use them as indicators on your connection, rather than finding the things that are giving stress and seeing them as indicators as disconnection.

For by seeing the little things and appreciating their existence, we let the wellbeing flow, and let go of the stress, letting it flow even more.

For many artists/composers/writers the trick of the trade is restrictions.

If they don't set themselves restrictions before beginning the creation they have too many options and the piece gets unfocused.

Spirit works the same and often the restrictions that we have in life, the boulders that we feel we have to plough through are there for a reason.

When we trust in the restrictions as well as the dream, then we can know that all will flow when it is time and the restrictions are simply there because too many choices could lead to no choice at all.

All is well and it is merely this moment that we need to focus on the creation of, the rest is unfolding as we go.

We may not be able to control other people, we may not be able to control outcomes and events, but it's comforting to know that in an ever unpredictable world, we can always control our thoughts.

It is an empowering moment to stop ourselves midway through a negative mental rant and CHOOSE to think a different thought.

To select a thought process and really think it with our whole selves until we feel better makes us feel alive and makes that moment sparkle with the possibilities.

That is how we consciously create moments and how positive days and created of those moments: it is simply remembering to choose a better feeling thought and then to fully think it.

A to-do list can trick our minds into thinking it's more important than play.

However, no matter what, in 20 years' time we will never look back and say "I really wish I'd done more of that to do list."

We will always say "I'm so glad I played."

When we remind ourselves of this every once and awhile, it's amazing the relief that comes with it.

We can read in so many articles or books how vital it is to listen to what our children are saying and talk to them about their feelings. In truth, listening goes deeper than that.

We can listen to a child express their upset about how they feel life is unfair and know for a fact that we do our best to keep life fair. But in fact, we have to listen to our child's heart, which is hurting for other reasons perhaps and is also feeling heavy from the thoughts the head is focused on.

Last, we have to listen to our children's spirits, which as positive beings, beg us to refocus on something better, to help shift to the better thoughts in life.

Yes, it is important to listen to our children, but keeping focused on yet another negative rant, will only confirm that for them more, listening to what's really going on, may mean we gently interrupt and refocus onto something better to help them make the shift.

Fun and play!

It's amazing what having some fun with our family can dissolve.

It's not just about playing for their pleasure, but for our own fun as well.

So often we feel like we have to be on top of everything and can't fully let go, as if we have to appear to be the ones who have it all under control, but by letting go and having fun with our children we can elevate beyond the need of anyone being in control.

We can treat them as the people they are and they can see us as the same.

It is as if we all float to the surface and can bob along the stream of life together, rather than go against the tide.

Whenever we have a problem and we simply state it and then let it go, resisting the urge to bang about at the problem over and over, we can trust that Source will offer a solution in some way or other and usually pretty quickly.

Therefore, rather than question what each day brings, and try to plan it and assess it, we can actually live each day as if it is the solution, even if we don't understand how, for within each day is the possibility for all our problems to be answered.

Oh, of course new problems may arise and their solutions might come about tomorrow. But today is full of answers.

All we have to do is trust that they are there and allow them to flow in and transform us.

Whereas re-watching things, re-visiting things, re-reading things, re-playing things can seem repetitive to us, for our children it can create healthy balance.

When a child returns to something they use to do or take part in they see it with new eyes having grown and expanded to a newer perspective.

A toddler will forget the toys they played with as a baby and will see them anew when they have them again.

A child will witness a different story reading the same book at three, six, or ten.

Life is progressively moving forward, but if we as adults assume that something we did ages ago is done and gone, then we miss the opportunity to enchant our children with it again, and strengthen a bond that was created with it the first time around.

As positive parents it is easy to think we have to allow our children the choice of everything.

True, we have to trust their instincts and listen to their voice, however if we feel by our own instincts that they are acting from a place of disconnection then sometimes the only thing that feels right is to gently place a hand on their shoulder and say

"Take your hand off the wheel for a bit, don't worry I'll drive".

We want our children to feel safe and secure and sometimes taking control of situations, not their spirits, gives them relief not a drive to rebellion.

It all depends on our intention and whether it comes from our heart or our mind.

Some days everything just seems to be a struggle.

No amount of preparation can keep you on time, things get dropped, spilt on, you feel overwhelmed and everything that comes out of your mouth turns out to be the wrong thing.

Off days happen, and in being aware of them we can sit back, stop, take a breather and refocus.

Often things start going awry when we are pushing too hard on something we think we need to do, and its Source's way of letting us know we need to lighten up.

The Law of Attraction amplifies our pushing and away we go. Therefore, if we reset the tone of the day and find a way of creating an atmosphere that rings out truer to ourselves, then everything can click back into place. Play, be spontaneous, surprise your kids and have fun.

The ride is more enjoyable with the foot a little lighter on the gas pedal anyway.

When we deeply appreciate various elements in our lives we open up a door within ourselves, allowing ourselves to feel deeper and be truer to ourselves.

Taking the moment, or the day, to truly appreciate our children, our family, our homes, even our favourite food or sunset, is a magical ingredient to being spiritually aware.

For when we open ourselves up to feeling deeper within ourselves, we wake ourselves up from the passive sleep of everyday activities, and in that awakening see the joys life has to offer.

We can trust in the tools we offer by example. Our children see everything we do, and more importantly feel everything we resonate.

When we are aware of how we feel, and follow through with our instincts, connection and avoidance of acting from places of feeling "off", our children see when things go smoothly and when we jive in life.

It is natural for them to want to feel good and when they see us working towards the same goal, they absorb our processes and it becomes their foundation.

When we get disconnected and acknowledge it, they see that too, understanding that life is a journey of feeling off and connected, going downstream and up and they retain that knowledge for their future.

When something becomes difficult, if an action suddenly causes stress and that tightness in your body that begs you to stop, then Stop.

When we try to push through the stress we simply create more.

However, when we stop, redirect our focus onto something else and then return to the original action, usually we see something we missed before, or we realize we were mistaken.

There is always some reason for the stress. It's the Source's way of asking ourselves to stand aside and take that moment.

The reason of Now or the process of how we got to this moment is irrelevant.

Rather it is what we do with each Now that sets up the next.

Often when we have a problem or are stressed in the moment we look for a reason for us being in that place and a purpose for feeling off.

However, if we shift to focusing on something that feels better, either appreciating something, imagining something and connecting to Source,

Then the Now becomes golden, our stress disperses and relief flows in.

We can all have a hidden tool box: The inner store room within us where we keep things that change how we feel.

It can be filled with ideas and dreams that we love to think, it can be songs that when we hear them we are launched to a new emotional state, it can be filled with images of those that we love and appreciate.

It can even be filled with activities such as running, dancing or gardening, that when we take part in them, we feel our souls almost leap for joy.

There are so many different things we have felt and experienced in life, when we remind ourselves of them, and take them out to play with them once again, we take control of how we feel, launching ourselves to a new feeling space, and a new NOW.

When life is going well we become unconscious of time, thinking that it will flow effortlessly forever.

But then a bump in the road will always appear and when it does we become incredibly conscious of time, worrying that the effect of the bump will last forever and nothing will ever be the same.

Life is an on-going stream of on again off again, connected, disconnected moments. When things aren't feeling at a jiving state, we simply need to relax, trust that it will pass, focus on what goes well and know that the hard time will make the new so much better, defining us and who we are to a deeper place.

Although it feels awful to have our children go through a rough patch of any kind, it helps to remind ourselves that they too will find their connection again, and it doesn't take as long as we ever worry it will.

All it takes is a moment and that is what life is made of.

Often when our children are acting a certain way we feel the urge to tell them to act a different way.

It can't be done.

However we are acting is a representation of how we are feeling. The feeling space of where we are at has to change before behaviour can.

Therefore, slowly and subtly work on changing the energy of the house.

Put on different movies or music, go to somewhere new or play a different game. Shift to creating the feeling you want and then it makes room for the new behaviour. Children always rise to the occasion.

The only thing we can offer our children are ourselves; our thoughts, our feelings, our dreams, our aspirations, our inspirations and our perspective.

No matter how much we would like to offer them the world on a silver platter, we have to trust in their own journeys and their own connection, so that they may create their own version of a silver platter as their life progresses.

In focusing in on offering the best version of ourselves, opportunities will present themselves that will create the best outcome for everyone.

Things don't have to be as serious as we make them out to be.

In other words, we don't actually have to stop the fun and "grow up" as we've been lead to believe.

When we stop the planning, the organizing, the attempting to predict and prevent and just allow to feel good, to have fun and to see where the winding road takes us, we live in the moment, we live the adventure and we live like our children, one step at a time.

Sometimes when children don't act as we wish, as a parent we feel helpless and confused about the right steps to take.

Do we demand different behaviour, let it go, or try to peacefully suggest other ways of being?

The first thing to look at is our own connection to Who We Really Are and to remember that when we feel off, we notice the offness of others more.

IF we connect ourselves first then we can see our children as their truest selves.

We also have to allow them to feel off, so they can find their own way back again.

When we are feeling true to ourselves we can trust our words and actions more. Rather than reacting in frustration we will be able to understand the deeper cause and help everyone reach for joy together.

What is going well?

It's an important question and one we ask too rarely.

So often our problems, or our children's problems, can become our focus and we bounce from one issue to another.

But when we stop to focus on what is flowing in our days, on what is working perfectly or on the little surprises that the day has offered that really lifted our hearts, we are reminded that all things are perfect and that things often go smoothly, even where we least expected.

It's amazing how much mental space we can give the last episode of our favourite TV show, a newspaper article or idle gossip.

It often goes un-noticed, yet round and round thru our heads it goes and in doing so creates a feeling space that matches it.

If we would just stop ourselves a few times a day, and use the time to reclaim ourselves, breathe, relax, appreciate and Be.

Then we would become more present in our days.

We can't teach our children about connection.

No matter how hard we try, words will not relay to them what deep down they naturally know.

We can only live it ourselves, be true to it ourselves and then create spaces of beauty, calm and openness to allow what is naturally within them to flow forth.

We don't need to force anything, simply create the space, ask, and then allow.

Our children will experience connection in whatever form is naturally within them.

It's so interesting when we see ourselves as the example for our children.

We can't expect them to listen,

if we don't listen.

We can't expect them to speak lovingly,

if we don't ourselves.

But most importantly, we can't expect them to be true to themselves,

to find time to listen to that inner source and to trust that it's good to feel good,

unless we shine with that inner truth ourselves.

Find the time to feel good.

When they feel "off", sometimes our children just need help to see things from a different perspective.

It's so easy to get frustrated when a child is feeling negative, however, sometimes we can simply offer them tools to shift their focus and they jump on board.

My favourite tool is to start a sentence off with an "at least."

At least I'm not alone, at least tomorrow's a new day, at least I am healthy etc.

It's a tool we can use for ourselves as well.

There are so many opportunities to say "no" to our children.

However, in doing so we not only limit them and keep them in a place of un-fulfillment, but we are saying no to ourselves as well, creating a negative block that says no as a habit rather than saving it for when something feels truly off.

Say yes as often as you can.

You will feel more alive and more open to all of life around you.

When something is bothering us, or when we want something to change, it is really a question of acknowledging it, offering it up to source, and then trusting the solution will come.

The more we puzzle over it, struggle with it, and focus on the problem the more we will see it in our lives.

By shifting focus to the solution, the more room we leave for the answer to just pop in.

And the answer Always pops in.

As parents it's vital to give our children room to try things out for themselves and how it feels to try them out.

Rather than trying to tell them how they should be,

sometimes it's best to sit back, remind them to focus on Who They Really Are

and more importantly who they want to be.

Life is about discernment and variety is important.

Breathe, relax, hold the picture of who your child is in your heart

and let it be.

In the pursuit of what we want,

either for our futures or of our children,

we often miss what we already have.

Live the life within you

and it will create the life before you.

Our children's perspectives, their beliefs, their joys can be influenced by ours, but are formed by them and how they see life.

It is a statement of Who They Really Are.

Therefore, if they feel off, we can offer them choices to help them feel better, but it's not up to us to make sure they feel better.

We can only be the shoulder to cry on,

the crutch to support them,

and the smiling face when they connect again.

What do you want?

Is something missing or do you want something to change?

We all have a tendency to ask for something we want, then ask and ask again.

It's a bit like ordering at a restaurant and then calling the server back over and over.

Recognize what you are wanting,

ask, and then let it go.

All will fall into place perfectly,

sometimes differently than expected,

but always perfectly and better than we could plan.

Words can often get us into a tangled mess.

As parents we often have so much information,

so many things we want our children to "get",

that we blab on and on creating a buzzing noise in our children's ears and not being understood.

If we attempt to not be ruled by fear of missed opportunity

and trust in communication by our own intention and example,

than the right words will come from us, always at the perfect time.

Giving birth is the ultimate lesson

on living life.

We can plan on how we want it to go,

*and we know that focusing our thoughts
create better outcomes.*

*However, the more we try to control the
process of "creation" or birth, the more
resistance we hold on to.*

*It is by letting go and allowing things to flow
without our input,*

*trusting that all is well and that our vision
will be manifested,*

*that we truly take part in the process rather
than trying to create it on our own.*

*It is always a co-creation involving us, our
baby, and the universe itself.*

At our children's core they are the truest form of genius according to their source and themselves.

If we see them as that, they can rise to it.

If we hold them up to a world made standard, they will never be able to thrive past that standard as we will always be there to see them as not meeting the mark.

I think we can all appreciate how that feels, where as often as parents we are held up to a marker.

Many a parent has shrieked

"I can't hear myself think!"

It is time to create a space in each of our days to "feel ourselves BE."

If we each take just a moment in the morning and a moment before bed to breathe, letting our bodies drop in sweet contentment of the moment and just BE, listening to Source's whispers, then we would find our days were filled with listening, laughter and life.

We wouldn't need to even worry about hearing our thoughts, as they would be heard all in the right time,

somewhere between BE-ing and Loving.

Be brave enough to say you're sorry to your children when you've done something that settles wrong with your own heart.

There is a freedom in not trying to be the perfect parent and in the honesty of admitting to it to our children.

It allows them the freedom to not be perfect all the time and to openly apologize for their own off moments.

No matter how many times we tell our children

how wonderful they are,

how special they are,

how beautiful they are,

it is only when we see them as such that they will truly believe us.

Therefore, take time to watch your children each day.

Appreciate who they are as they play, cherish them as they walk outside, marvel at them when they laugh, love them as they speak about their day.

When we take the time to appreciate Who Are Children Are, we are telling them how amazing they are, without the need of words and offering them the basement for

true self esteem.

It is worth the effort to feel good.

It is worth taking a moment to shift focus onto something that makes you feel better, rather than follow the spiral of reaction to reaction to reaction to what is happening in front of you.

When you remind yourself that it is worth it, that when you feel good,

when you dance,

when you sing, when you see what the good side to every coin,

things just line up better,

life clicks into place and even in the rough patches you see the magic solution to spin it round, then you take the moment to smile, breathe and let it all flow in.

It never feels good to think our children may be heading down a road we "disapprove" of.

When we trust our children will shine their own light and we need not worry, we set them free.

In setting them free to be themselves, we set ourselves free.

Sure often we feel programmed, we feel like we aren't doing our job right if we don't worry: if we aren't mother hens.

But there isn't any greater feeling then saying the words,

"I trust you. I believe in you.

You are so great at being you!"

That is the greatest parenting feeling possible.

Worry, apprehension, criticism, they are all acts of Fear.

Fear isn't a part of the job.

All we are called to be is Love givers.

Just as each type of plant requires different forms of care to thrive

(direct sunshine, more water, a song)

so too do children.

There are no generalized rules that cover everyone.

What feels good to me, doesn't always feel good to you.

Some children thrive with extended breastfeeding, some might not, some children thrive in school, others do not, some children love the country, others the city, some play with dolls, and others ride bikes.

There are no generalized rules for any of us, and that is the beauty of life.

We aren't cranking out robots, uniform models, we are taking part in a blissful journey of individualism, where each of us gets to define ourselves daily and express our differences and opinions.

Trust in your own instinct, your own inner voice.

If something feels Off: it is.

If something feels On: it is.

If something defies logic, yet feels so right that it seems blissful, go for it.

We should always encourage our children to follow their hearts and we owe it to them to listen to their hearts as well in matters concerning them.

Become a family of hearts,

where each heart has a voice and a common goal to be listened to.

For petty desires of all may clash, but hearts are made to intermingle with each other.

Words are deceptive indicators of how our children are doing.

We ask "how are you feeling?" "How was your day?" "Are you alright?" and expect our children to honestly be able to express their answer from the heart.

Would we be able to reply to the answer? Wouldn't we constantly have a plethora of elements that would affect it?

We would take into consideration what the other person would like to hear, we would also have a lot of things going on we wouldn't necessarily be aware of right away, so we might blame it on something that wasn't the problem in the first place.

No, words are deceptive indicators.

It is far more precise to watch our children. Do they skip? Do they laugh? Do they act as Who They Really Are?

And as parents we have to learn to see them as who they really are, not who we think we know them to be!

Our children deserve to have us present when we are with them.

It doesn't mean we have to live our life around them all the time, it is reasonable and in fact vital to have time to explore our own passions and thoughts, however when we are spending time with them it is vital to give them our focus.

So often our chattering minds can work over time while our children are telling us about their day, sharing a story or even making a complaint about their siblings. We get in the habit of having such a long to do list that we have to multi task through every conversation.

But when we don't offer our attention we forget to offer ourselves and our children are left dealing with a paper thin version of ourselves.

This then becomes the example we offer and we receive the mirror image of it.

Be yourself, be in the moment and enjoy your children's company and let the love exchange spark the family fire.

Be aware of references like "what children like" or "what a child needs" or any other generalizing remark concerning what's best for ALL children.

Each child is an individual, with their own likes, dislikes, habits, talents, desires, dreams and most of all, Spirits.

When we make sweeping comments about them we limit them to being "children".

When we see them as themselves, simply inexperienced and dare I say shorter than us, we empower them to be themselves and to speak with their own voice.

We each personally feel uncomfortable when people try to assume things about us based on any generalization, why should it be any different for our children.

At our core we are pure positive energy. When we feel good, when we feel better, we are connected to who we really are.

Many people will tell you that you can't feel good when bad things happen as that is simply denial. Yet feeling good isn't always about dancing in the streets or having a huge smile on our faces.

Rather in all moments of our life we are faced with options of reaction.

One choice will always feel better than the other, one will always feel more inherently like ourselves, and when we make that choice, no matter what the situation, it will always feel good.

When we act as Who We Are we glow from within and when we encourage our children to choose their actions based on that positive gut feeling we are offering them freedom and a life of wellbeing.

Sometimes we suddenly feel the urge to relate some wisdom to our children and when we approach them it feels like they don't hear us at all.

At this point a good imagination is a great tool. Before approaching our children when we have the "instinct" to relate something through words if we imagine how we would feel if someone told us the same thing we will sense whether saying it is truly the right action to take.

Often, we may find that even relating it to ourselves is rather boring to hear and we can understand our children tuning out.

Then we can simply offer the request that our children comprehend the concept and allow the right way, time and opportunity to come up and the universe will always provide without talking our children's ears off.

By using our imagination to see the world and ourselves through our children's eyes (and ears) we can feel our way to the best approach and to what they need.

It's alright to let it go.

We don't have to get it right, we don't have to have it all under control, and we don't have to appear that we know what we're doing.

Life is about the journey of it all, the off and the on of it all and when we let go we can laugh and play just as our children do.

Often we can criticize ourselves so much we hold it all in, trying to be in control of everything we experience.

But in truth, when we try to control ourselves and hold it all in, than we become a dam to our natural spirits trying to break free.

The only thing we need to watch is our connection.

When we feel the freedom of connection, we can let go and enjoy each moment in itself, without worry of the future, or concern based on the past.

Connect, laugh, breath, and trust that all is wellbeing flowing forth.

To appreciate our child's perspective as much as our own is a developed gift that is worth putting the effort into.

While our children live with us they live with our perspective and often that outlook becomes the dominant one of the house, unless we're careful.

When we remember that our beliefs and view of life are our own, created from our life experience, then we shouldn't encourage our children to simply pick up where we leave off.

Rather, we should remind ourselves that their outlook is often different from our own. Their lives are leading them to a different perspective, in fact, from the moment of their conception they were observing and creating their own viewpoint and that has lead them to where they are now.

A mutual recognition of holding unique personal preferences is a magic ingredient to a happy home.

Often when people hear the concept of not using discipline, they assume you let your children do whatever they want.

It is not a question of letting yourself become a slave, rather as a Spiritually Aware Parent it is to see your children as the same as yourself.

We are all on equal terms and deserve the same treatment as each other.

If something bothers us, we can admit it, and talk about it, working together to find a solution.

If something bothers our children, they too can bring it to the family's attention.

The concept of a family as an orchestra, each with their own instrument, equal in beauty and perfection that needs the conductor simply to play together as a group; that is the perfect solution in place of discipline.

So often a young child will have a tantrum or act out of control simply because he doesn't understand what is happening around him or he senses unsettledness in the house and it disturbs him.

Our children rarely "act out" consciously.

They usually don't have a plan how to spiral in behavior and it is definitely unusual that they feel/act the way they do just to get to us.

When we believe in our children's innocence, and see life from their perspective we can comprehend how overwhelming it can be sometimes.

Life is constantly flowing,

and with the growth of our children,

that stream moves fast.

When I look back at my children's lives and my relationships with them from when they were in my arms for the first time I have a deep sense of the wellbeing that flows for us all.

For although I don't nurse my eldest, or change her, or carry her anymore, when I think of her, the essence is still the same as that baby, no matter how our roles have changed for each other.

Savor the moment in time, savor the Now, for things progress and change, they flow in with the same joy,

but they do progress.

I don't know about you, but almost all of my spiritual beliefs and experiences have derived from my own thoughts, instincts, inspired moments of reading or being at the right place at the right time.

Very rarely am I "told" something by someone and it become concrete in my heart and head, no matter how strongly I'm told.

It is the same with our children. Surrounding our children is the same wellbeing and inspirational Source that flows towards us.

By trusting in that source for ourselves, we must trust in it for them as well.

Source will occasionally use us as inspiration for our children, but only at the right time.

It is worth the effort to feel good.

*It is worth taking a moment to shift focus
onto something that makes you feel better,
rather than follow the spiral of reaction to
reaction to what is happening in front of you.*

*When you remind yourself that it is worth it,
that when you feel good, when you dance,
when you sing, when you see what the good
side to every coin,*

things line up just better,

life clicks into place

*and even in the rough patches you see the
magic solution to spin it round.*

*Then you take the moment to smile, breathe
and let it all flow in.*

Although it's easy to feel our back go up when our children disagree with us, seeing life from their eyes offer a better feel good option.

Our children are constantly defining themselves, deciding who they are and who they want to become.

By stating their opinions they are making a clear statement about themselves.

Give them the validation to like different things and believe different things then you and you offer them freedom to be themselves.

However, validate yourself by not hiding what you like and believe either.

To thine own self be true... and may our children be true to themselves.

To be a spiritually aware parent is to take a moment within the chaos of the day to check in with yourself and connect to that truest part of yourself.

To be a spiritually aware parent is to take a moment before reacting to your child's behavior and connect to the truest part of them.

It is to act, not react,

to Be and not always Do,

it is to Trust and not doubt,

and to love rather than to act from worry and fear.

Be well, happy and thrive, for wellbeing flows all around us always.

All we have to do is stop and let it flow in.

Sometimes it helps to take stock of how the feeling space of our homes resonates.

In the general pace of day to day living, sometimes the essence of our house can become muddled and by taking a moment to sit and let it flow over you, you can get a sense of what the default feeling space is.

Is there a sense of joy and laughter that rings through the walls,

or do you sense frustration and tension?

Every home goes through good and bad periods, but by being aware of the negative you can shift your focus to the feeling space you want to echo through your house and let it flow in.

Quiet should be more than a time without noise, for often the chatter can come from within.

Quiet in its truest sense is to relax into that inner space, when you feel your head lighten in the peace of it.

We often say that it's hard to find quiet when there are children about, but at any time and in any place it is possible to close our eyes, put attention on the quiet within, distract ourselves from the noise without and find peace again.

The art of appreciation is often considered as being grateful or shifting our thoughts to being thankful for things in our life.

This is true to a point, being grateful/thankful opens us up to consideration and interaction with others, it reminds us of what we have and shifts focus from what we want or what we don't have.

However, the art of appreciation is slightly different. When we appreciate something or someone, we savor them to our core.

Appreciation is a feeling more than a thought. Our heart swells, we smile, and we feel better.

What a lovely thing it is to truly appreciate the people in our lives.

To relish the very essence of them.

To enjoy the very sight of them and to let that enjoyment overtake our entire selves.

For while we appreciate and love we can't experience negative emotion.

Resistance describes the pushing against the flow of wellbeing.

Perhaps there is no other position in life that can create more resistance than that as a parent.

We want to control meal times and being on time (and it stresses us out when we're late), we want to control how our children "turn out", we want to control their experience and we want to control their interactions with others.

The more we control the more resistance and pushing against we create.

And you always get what you push against.

Therefore, by reminding ourselves that "all is well" and allowing our children's story to unfold,

resistance is released and life flows in.

It's noticing that punch in the stomach feeling after reading something that upsets you, or savoring it when your heart skips a beat out of pride for your child.

It's tapping your fingers on the table when you need a moment to shift quickly, or tears coming to your eyes out of relief.

Our bodies, our minds, and our heart full of emotion blend together seamlessly and when we notice their indicators we can savor the ones that feel wonderful and shift from the ones that feel awful, taking control of our emotional space and of our days:

acting rather than reacting.

When you feel stuck,

appreciate the stuckness.

When you feel frustration or aggravation
appreciate the offness for it all serves as a
bouncing off place for newness of life.

The Off makes the On more wonderful

and in appreciating it,

you'll never feel stuck for long.

Small things can make us more in the moment and present parents:

checking email/facebook less in the day, and building a fort instead,

waiting 15 minutes later to do the dishes and sitting to read a few books with your child on your lap,

focusing thoughts and writing a to-do list of things to think, write, surf or talk about after everyone is in bed and just be-ing with your family.

The affect of just one of these actions is amazing as it reshifts the entire house and your entire perspective of priorities and what feels wonderful.

Have fun; it's what life is all about.

We all want to give our children the best childhoods possible.

We plan, we ponder, we worry as we try to create the best opportunities for them (you know, the ones we felt we never had).

However, it's important to wonder-

Isn't it likely that the day to day life we are offering is EXACTLY what they need and what they came for?

It can bring such relief to remember that our children chose us, not only for who we are, but for what we offer in each day and where we are in this time.

Therefore, we shouldn't worry about what future we can carve out for them, rather we should trust that today is perfect and relish in it.

Perception is what decides the life we live and defines who we are.

If we aren't happy in our life at the moment, often shifting our perspective onto different elements of it tells a different story and therefore allows a shift in our reality to take place.

So too is it with our children and when we attempt to see the world through their eyes rather than our own, we can understand them so much better.

We can also often appreciate our own life more by seeing it through their beautiful eyes of innocence.

Within you is a powerhouse of tools to create a better life for you and your children.

Often the magic happens when we allow ourselves to feel good no matter what, simply by shifting focus on to other things than the problems at hand.

When we feel off, we can feel better by focusing on things that are going well, and if others are acting in ways that feel off, we can focus on who we know them to really be and allow room for that person to show up.

Whenever we focus on problems,

they are all we see.

When we focus on solutions,

they are what we get.

There is so much more than what is here before us, so much more.

All around us there are powerful things at work,

more powerful than broken cars, late bills, sick children, or just feeling fed up.

Under, around, and within, is a system of unseen powers that when we remind ourselves of its existence the problems seem to shrink smaller and smaller.

Stress and worry are relatives of Fear, and fear can't survive in the presence of Love or in the remembrance of that inner and outer power.

Love, love, love and feel good.

Everything is well and perfect.

When someone we love and care for is going through an off time, it's easy to slip into worry, concern and stress about them.

In doing so we think we're helping, but in fact we're doing two things that can't offer support.

First we risk losing our own connection if we spend too long staring at the problem

and second by seeing the offness in them we take a picture of it and use it as the reference point of who they are, thereby giving them no room to grow and change from the experience.

The best help we can offer is to focus on the truest part of them, and look only at the best.

Acknowledging the problem,

but focused on the soul-ution.

Things don't have to be as serious as we make them out to be.

In other words, we don't actually have to stop the fun and "grow up" as we've been lead to believe.

When we stop the planning,

the organizing,

the attempting to predict and prevent

and just allow to feel good, to have fun and to see where the winding road takes us,

we live in the moment, we live the adventure and we live like our children,

one step at a time.

We can recall memories by the strangest things.

Smells, sounds, tastes, and then there's the sixth sense, they all trigger the feeling, or energy, of the time that past.

The same sort of feeling spaces, and memories, are being formed for us and our children daily.

When we are aware of this we can consciously create the feeling of the day.

We can also line up the feeling space of tomorrow, by focusing on the feeling or energy we wish to feel in the future.

By using our imaginations and actually putting ourselves in the feeling we want, rather than being in the feeling of without it by default, we create a pre-memory that our senses can rise to.

The idea of life isn't to disguise it with rose colored glasses all the time, rather it's to be aware of what glasses we are looking through at each moment, and when we don't like how things are looking, know that we have the choice to pick another pair.

Life is about perspective and although sometimes it's difficult, with a little bit of scrambling around a subject, we can usually find another way of seeing it.

Look for the perspective that makes you feel better, tell the lighter story, and life will indeed look rosier.

Change is inevitable.

It is the process of life moving forward, of expansion and growth, of newness, that calls forth life and allows us to experience every aspect of who we are and who we want to be.

So often as parents we want to hold off change.

While our children run for the new moment, we want to pull them back, trying to linger in the moment just a little longer.

Breathe and relax, for sometimes it isn't a leap, rather a two steps forward, one step back sort of growth.

Often a child will leap forward, and then turn back and run into our arms again.

Cherish the moment, savor it, and then honor the change.

Plan only when it feels wonderful to plan, otherwise simply put the focus on creating a beautiful feeling day in the moment.

For there is nothing that feels more wonderful than an unplanned perfect moment.

When suddenly, and without warning, the universe delivers something that makes everything else make perfect sense,

and we couldn't have been so touched by it if we'd seen it coming.

The only thing we can offer our children is ourselves;

our thoughts, our feelings, our dreams, our aspirations, our inspirations and our perspective.

No matter how much we would like to offer them the world on a silver platter, we have to trust in their own journeys and their own connection,

so that they may create their own version of a silver platter as their life progresses.

In focusing in on offering the best version of ourselves, opportunities will present themselves that will create the best outcome for everyone.

Oh, I hate slippery days!

You know the days when a tiny negative thought creeps in, and then another follows, and then another.

Before you know it, law of attraction has built up steam and you feel overwhelmed by your own thoughts and the frustrating circumstances they've created.

It feels like slipping on ice and not being able to find balance.

Once you know you're slipping, just stop.

Focus on one thing, for a moment. Focus on the sound of the wind, or the water as you wash your hands, focus on your child's laughter appreciating every ripple.

Just as the Law of Attraction took hold of the negative thought, so it will on the positive.

Let feeling good slowly relieve you. Build your thoughts on things that make you feel better.

Better feeling thoughts are the grit to a slippery day.

Our children often have heroes: people they admire or strive to be like.

However, we often give up this time of idolatry as we get older.

Perhaps we miss out on something.

For the purpose of a "hero" is to recognize something in them that you see a glimmer of within yourself, and to use it as a shortcut to enhance that gift within you.

This can help in moments of disconnection, for when we ask how our hero would respond in a situation we open ourselves up to different options, and in doing so can find better connection to ourselves.

Source, the Universe, is a wonderful example of a good parent.

We can ask, and ask, and ask, but the universe will never just listen to what we say and go yes, yes, yes.

Rather it parents/gives to our truer selves, looking to the deeper need.

When we are connected to Who we Really Are, jiving to our inner calling, then what we want naturally flows towards us.

When we aren't connected...

and dare I say whiny...

the universe holds off a bit, saying

"I don't think you really need that right now."

Often people think that when we make feeling good our main priority that we are being "selfish".

But it's interesting isn't it?

For if we aren't taking care of our own connection, and insuring that we are acting from our Truest of Selves, then we can't help anyone

and if we don't make it our priority because we've been told it is selfish, then we are sacrificing ourselves to make sure the world revolves around the ones that consider it selfish...

which make them the selfish ones, doesn't it?

It's a simple decision to Feel Good anyway and not let life decide how we react.

There is always some angle to a problem that will bring a touch of sweet relief.

All it takes is looking for it.

Would you rather be praised for what you do or Who you are?

In a time when people are constantly questioning praising children for their efforts, perhaps it's time we shift to focusing on Who They Are.

I love to tell my children how well they are doing, or saying "I'm so proud of Who you are" before bed.

I love the feeling it gives to me, to focus on their inner work, rather than their outer accomplishments.

Oh yes, I also congratulate them when they achieve something on a physical level, but it always feels so right to praise the inner, and let the outer be a reflection of what is going on within.

You don't have to run the course of any feeling state.

Sometimes when we are frustrated, or angry or simply feeling off we hold off feeling better because we feel there is a time lapse we need to fulfill.

We think we need to time to "get over it." There is no time that needs to be served.

A change of thought process can be immediate, and it supposedly takes a mere 17 seconds of a shift in thought to have another thought come a support it and then another and another... making you feel a whole lot better.

Therefore, even if it feels too quick of shift, feel better as soon as possible.

Your day, and family, will thank you.

It's a safe bet that all of us would wish for more time, stress free, quality time to play and laugh with our children, for nothing is better than in the moment, quality play time.

However, so often we run around, placing other things as the priority over playing.

It's as if we feel there are so much more important things in life than feeling good and we want our children to believe it too.

Our children will never believe it.

They would much rather feel good and play than to get to bed on time, or than to rush out the door without a few laughs.

Perhaps there's a compromise. Perhaps we *should all chose to find time to play, even before doing some of the things we "need" to do.*

Play and fun doesn't have to be the dessert after eating all of our Brussels sprouts, rather a sweet afternoon snack!

Parenting has so many wonderful stages and in being aware of them we can appreciate each one to the fullest.

First there's the Provider stage when they are an infant, then the Enabler stage for a toddler as we help them explore and find new ground, then the Inspirer for when the world has become taken for granted to them and we can reinvent perspectives.

Around 5 or 6 we become a bit of a Guide, showing them the options of being and living, and then suddenly we find ourselves as the Silent Consultant and Supporter, trusting in everything they are as they approach their challenges and experiences.

We shift through these stages, and occasionally revisit them when needed.

And in the co co-creation between each child and parent, is the perfect weaving, with them providing us with the stages we need too.

Trust in wellbeing.

No matter what comes your way, no matter how stressed or complicated life feels at the moment, you can trust that wellbeing abounds for you.

Take a break, throw the covers over your head, think of something else, toss the problem out to the universe and see if it can send back a picture of it from a different angle.

You are not alone in this and all the forces in the world are working to create the perfect life for you.

Problems define what you want and who you are.

Coming out of them creates the better Now.

As parents it often feels we are constantly on duty.

No matter where we go, no matter what we do it is hard to drop into that inner space, without quickly jumping out wondering if everyone is alright, everyone is safe and everything is taken care of.

Find a time to breathe and relax into wellbeing.

Even if it's just before bed, find a time where the music within you can sing, and eek it out that little bit longer before you stop yourself to ask *"what was that?"*

Go within, so that all may be well outside of yourself.

*When you sense your child needs something,
leave words as a last resort.*

*Trust that your instincts will show you how
to offer opportunities for your child to shift,
or at least see the differences in ways of
being and attraction points.*

*Sometimes, it can be as simple as changing
the feeling space of the home, even through
putting on a quiet, focused movie or music.*

*Change of pace, focus, and feeling spaces
always provide your child a chance to make a
shift, all on their own.*

Are our children reflections of us?

What we notice in our children at any given time is a reflection of where we stand in that moment, therefore, if we are feeling irritated, than we notice the things that bug us, or if we are in joy, we enjoy all of their actions.

Also, the things that we often worry about in our children often reflect our own weaknesses. If we worry they will fall victim to peer pressure, it's often because we think too much of other people's opinion ourselves, if we think they can't stick to something, it's usually because we have problems seeing things through.

However, we can also be a reflection to them, which is where living as example is so valid.

When we try to be the change we want to see, we can let go of worry and trust in our inner reflection to us and everyone else.

Everyone gets stressed, upset, worried, frustrated, and even depressed.

By being aware of how we feel, we can be honest with ourselves, name the emotion and then ask ourselves how long we want to stay in that feeling space.

When we decide we want to feel better we can start shifting perspectives to focus on things that we appreciate, things that make us feel good, things that distract us and slowly get a connected footing.

Then the law of attraction will pick up on it and everything will go a whole lot better.

What an exciting thing for our children to be told: that they are not wisps in the wind feeling things at random, but that they're emotions serve a purpose and they can help themselves feel better by what they think about all day long.

Your life is in this Now.

When we focus too much on what has gone before and the why's, where's and how it could have gone differently, we spend our time regurgitating the same experiences, and never moving on.

When we focus on the future, we are left at the end of the day with depleted versions of dreams, and added stress and worry.

Spend some time each day appreciating and reveling in your Now.

Feel your breath, hear your heart, and let yourself shift to the broader perspective, where answers flow and you feel your way to a place that makes perfect sense for this moment.

Then, and only then, can we truly be in a present moment parenting position and really hear/feel what our children need.

We don't have to have all the answers.

In fact it's better that we don't.

For when we think we can answer every question, or have our parenting ways set in stone, we build a fortress around us, cutting us off from the expanding, living, breathing, flowing experience.

It's alright for our children to know we don't have all the answers.

It's ok for them to see themselves as part of the ever growing, changing journey.

For as they watch us grow and change and improve as parents, they will see that it's alright for them to constantly be growing and changing and that they too...

don't need to have all the right answers.

When we see our children acting unlike themselves

it is because they don't feel like themselves and when we look at it from a different perspective

we can find ways of changing their daily patterns or surroundings to help them find their connection again.

Visitors, vacations, special occasions are all examples of things that can make children feel uncomfortable within their own skin and often "off" behavior will follow.

When we can understand their perspective and situation the behavior stops simply being "off" to us and rather becomes an indicator for us to help them find a quiet moment to reconnect.

Negative emotions give us physical indicators.

It's an interesting experience to note when we feel extra tired or are fighting getting sick to see if we're emotionally feeling well or if we are disempowering ourselves with self-defeating brain chatter.

When we are aware of how we are feeling we can boost our energy by focusing on something that feels better,

sparking thoughts within ourselves that make us smile,

appreciate

or feel a sense of awe.

I promise to see only the best of you and expect only the best of you my darling one.

I may sometimes seem surprised when you do something that doesn't come from Who You Really Are, but at least I won't assume that is everything you are.

We all make mistakes, it's what life is about.

For when we make mistakes and then the opportunity comes to make them again and we choose not to, the relief and bliss of that moment is phenomenal.

Life is in the living and being of it all.

You are a wondrous, wonderful and adventurous being and no matter what that is who I love you as.

When our actions and Who We Really Are match up it is indescribable joy, when they don't it can hurt a lot.

I will hold constant faith that you feel more joy than pain your whole life, but no matter what, when I think of you,

I will see you as Who You Really Are,

the rest is simply experiments in feeling off and on.

We all have times when we just can't get in the grove of being the parents we want to be.

The house can ring out with frustrations and upset, rather than the happy, joyous burble we dream of.

We need to let it go and make it all part of the process.

When there's a shift in the energy of the house, it's usually because of new vantage points. Our children are constantly gaining new experiences and new perspectives and in doing so, bring those into the mixing pot of the family.

When we shift focus from the things we don't like, and focus on the things we appreciate, when we take the time to care for feeling spaces and shift them to the gentler, peaceful, joyous ones, when we find those hidden moments to connect with our children and ourselves, then slowly we can proactively be the example of people, who grow, change and shift to the better feeling space.

We can't tell our children how to be spiritually aware.

Rather it is how we are ourselves.

Sure, we will talk about it, as it is our perspective, but it's not usually our words that will hit our children's core.

Rather it is our actions, our approach and what we fill our lives with.

The books on our shelves, the music that fills rooms, the pictures on the wall,

they all set up an atmosphere that our children may notice, but may not.

Words aren't the best tool to use.

Rather we can let ourselves flow through things that make us feel good, and perhaps, the universe will use them to light our children up as well.

There's no rush to get it done.

There's no time limit on learning how to be the parent we want to be, or the deepest version of ourselves.

In fact, we never get it done.

Life is ongoing, and parenting is all part of the journey.

No matter how much we give, our children will only reap from it what they need to.

From their perspective, they will only see and hear what is a vibrational match to Who They Really Are, so the best approach is always to be true to Who We Really Are.

When we focus on being true to who we are, then the rest falls into place.

The more positive we feel, the wider our perspective and the more options we see.

The more options we see, the more ways the universe can assist us along the way.

As we run around, in our set ways, thinking in our patterns, feeling everything to a point, it is sometimes hard to grasp how our children can be filled with so much zest and joy over even just a trip to the grocery store.

There is always that thought in the back of our heads that tells us to stop them from expressing their boundless joy in a public place.

But when we relax and watch them with new found wonder rather than let it rub us the wrong way because of what people may think,

when we remember that they've got it right, then they have taught us a valuable lesson: Life is supposed to be FUN.

It is Fun to break the patterns, it is exhilarating to see the different angle, it is exciting to have ice cream!

Life is an adventure in the making and our children make sure they are always there to remind us that it is so.

We should never be too willing to speak to our children about spiritual/metaphysical things,

only ever ready.

For they are experiencing, perceiving and creating their journey and only at the perfect time for them will anything we can say about what they already know on deeper levels connect and make any sense to them.

In the meantime, it is our own spiritual life, our own striving to be the truest version of Who We Really Are,

that serves as example and when we get to the point of talking about unseen matters with our children, it will ring true to them as they have witnessed it by watching us.

When we feel off and we choose to feel better by appreciating our children,

one way to jump on board is to watch them play and appreciate their laughter, their imaginations, their energy, their eyes twinkling, their smiles.

However, sometimes, when we aren't an energy match to our children, even these things can seem to not hit to our core and help us connect.

A great way to become a "vibrational match" to our children is to go somewhere quiet, and appreciate the inner being of our children:

to call Who They Really Are up in our minds and see the world through their eyes, just for a moment.

When we can see life through their eyes, then when we are in the same room with them, we can appreciate all that they are in front of us...and that always makes us feel better!

We do not create our own reality by making plans or even in knowing what we "want"

(Often we can only know glimpses, like shadows, of what we really desire deep down).

Rather "reality" (and I use the term loosely) is created from the feeling space we resort to the most each day.

It is the way we respond to the needs of our children and those around us,

the way we act or react, the way we see life, and how we appreciate each moment, the way we look and expect each small miracle and marvel at each twist in the road,

rather than moan or take things for granted, that defines us and sets our "proclivity."

Each day, each moment offers a new opportunity to reset that viewpoint and create a better reality for ourselves-

not for what we get in the future

but for the joy, satisfaction and bliss of each new moment.

Our instincts, or inner voice, regarding any given subject, may often go against the logical argument,

and may sometimes sound irrational when voiced out loud,

but, no matter what, it is vital to follow them and stay true to our hearts.

For within us is all the knowledge of the unseen universe and it expands beyond terms of past or future.

Instincts will never use past references to what has been

or our fears of the future to argue its point.

Rather it will provide us with

a sense of relief,

a sense of "rightness"

when we consider its suggestion.

It is the simple thing of requesting and allowing.

Sometimes our children are going through a rough patch,

teething, growing, learning,

and we want to do anything in our power to make it better for them.

Often we can end up running around like headless chickens, trying anything and everything and causing chaos in the process.

In the simple act of making the request to the universe and then allowing an answer to flow in,

we release the pushing against the problem and put trust in the flow of wellbeing that is ever working to make life beautiful.

When we allow, it is amazing the small solutions that arise

and always at the perfect time.

Our children's journeys

have twists and turns that we as parents can't imagine the outcome of,

just as we can never imagine the detailed outcome of our own.

Rather than trying to predict and protect them from all potential dangers,

it is better to stand behind them the whole way, supporting their decisions,

trusting in their deep knowledge,

and offering them a helping hand and words that remind them of how loved they are.

Off and On, Off and On....

Sometimes something will feel so ON, so perfectly aligned, SO the right thing to do, that every part of us will have to do it.

Sometimes, things feel so Off, either one thing will feel so Off we just can't bring ourselves to do it, or everything feels off, so that nothing feels right.

That's Spiritual Awareness,

that's spiritual tools.

When things feel off, life won't flow when we force it, even if we want it really badly.

The only thing to do is to take a step back, breathe and find a way to connect again.

When things are On, it comes from Source, it's lined up and ready for the relishing,

so love every minute of it, savor it and let the life Roll in.

This is a practical thing our children can grasp, for they like nothing better than to feel good!

As an aware parent it is a wonderful experience to watch our children grow and expand, and find ways of expressing their deepest joys.

To hear their laughter,

as not only a nice moment,

but as an indicator that they are reveling in their truest selves.

To see off behavior as an indicator of bad feeling,

and a need to feel better.

To live on this journey with them,

not trying to squeeze them into yesterday's shoes,

but to offer them choices to find the best fitting option for their newest perspective on this road of life.

As parents there is usually a back log of things we mean to tell our children, (everything from the facts of life, to be true to yourself, to when you grow up don't drink and drive.)

We spend our day with mental conversations going on in our heads telling us things we should "make sure" they know.

We have to let it go a bit.

For when we do, when we let go, we have made the request for the information to pass through our lips and we allow the perfect time to convey it.

We can banter so much our children hear us as white noise, but when we speak when the perfect time arises, they hear it like music to their ears and the true meaning speaks volumes to them.

Trust...everything always comes at the right time.

Have you ever watched a toddler draw?

They create with no intention, but look at the paper with wonder when they sees what wonderful thing has appeared.

As we get older we tend to reverse that, we draw with intention,

but are harsh on our final work, saying it's not how we wanted it.

Although we can often create moments in our lives out of pure intention,

perhaps if we were to let go and draw first,

we would be surprised and overjoyed to see the wonderful things we had created and enjoy them in their manifestation,

rather than disappointed in being different then we expected.

Each choice we make is like a stone thrown in the water,

each bring different ripple effects when we throw it.

It's not only the big choices,

such as what school, or when to wean,

rather it is that split second choice of whether to react or to Act,

to lose it or to laugh,

to smile or to scream.

The ripples of a day when we've chosen to feel good in all those forks in the road,

when we've chosen relief over strife,

those ripples send musical vibrations from the soul,

and our spirits sing out for the feeling of such sweet relief.

I don't want my children to behave.

I don't want them to meet the mark,

to toe the line.

I'm not saying I want them to behave badly or to run wild in public, rather I want them to Be.

I want to enjoy their company and for them to enjoy mine.

I want to have fun and for them to have fun, and not to feel insecure or self conscious the way that children who run wild often do.

I'm not a lion tamer. I don't need to control my crew.

Rather, I can offer them the tools that make things go easier, the tools that I offer myself.

We all feel OFF sometimes.

But no matter what, they can know, we're in this together.

I won't squash them, they won't fear me. Rather, blissfully and merrily we will go downstream together.

We live our parenting days looking for ways to help bring sparkle to our children's eyes, knowing full well that in the end, only they can light the flame.

Therefore, rather than trying to play catch up and make our children happy,

even when they are disconnected, we are better off providing them with the tools to make happiness for themselves.

It's a bit like teaching them to fish for a life time rather than giving one fish for the day.

So laugh with them, play with them, and create a joyful life,

but if it feels off to you, or you feel like you are giving too much of yourself,

take the indicator from the universe that says it's time for your child to expand themselves, and learn the processes to achieve a happy heart.

Focus on the things that go well.

Remember the happy moments of each day rather than the stressful.

Breathe easy with the sweetness of each kiss from your child,

rather than tense up with every tantrum,

savour every laugh rather than harp on every mistake.

How you feel does matter, and it is what carries through to the next day.

So if you don't feel like feeling good,

if you just can't make it fit,

then focus on the things that go well,

even if it's just the simplest thing,

and breathe easier each moment at a time.

The feeling of pride for our children is one of the most blissful experiences we can ever attain.

Our hearts swell, we catch our breath and we see them in that moment as the truest versions of themselves.

Why is it then, that we often find ourselves trapped in the habit of looking at their faults or fearing for their choices?

If being proud feels so wonderful why not spend the moments looking for things to be proud of?

Our children don't even have to know we're doing it,

but by changing our outlook on our children's behaviour we will not only feel better, walking around in that blissful state,

but by putting focus on the wellness of it all, the more wellness will be created.

Sometimes our children run a course of feeling unlike themselves, or simply off.

We as parents can recognize these periods by when they get aggravated or frustrated easily, hurt themselves often, or seem to constantly be fighting being sick or tired.

We all feel off sometimes and it's always nice to feel we're not alone.

When we offer help, such as giving them some cuddle time, a quiet space to read and think, or a quiet bath, we offer them spaces to shift how they feel.

When someone is feeling disconnected, it is like they've fallen in a hole. It does no good for us to only offer sympathy and support where they are NOW, confirming how Off everything is, and it does no good to stand far away only concerned in our own connection for that can never feel good.

Rather, we can stand at the edge, holding out our hand and all it takes is for them to grab it and we can work together to find that perfect connection place.

It is often hard to remember that we are not in charge of our children's journey or how they feel each day.

We can take their connection to Who They Really Are so seriously that we try to make them feel good when in truth they feel bad.

As parents all we can do is offer them tools to feel better.

We can help them appreciate the life they have, trust in wellbeing that flows all around us, and have faith in the inherent goodness and brilliance of who they are within.

By practicing going within and connection ourselves we can be an example of the tools we offer,

by admitting to our disconnected moments we show that life is an on and off again process.

Trust where you've gotten to and how far you have come.

All things in our lives have led up to this point.

Wants, desires, dreams and preferences have been made; we are deciding what feels good to us, and who we really are.

Everything is perfect.

This next moment will be a bouncing off for yet another part of the journey, and the journey is always more important than the destination.

Cherish the good in each moment.

For life is an ever flowing stream and we gently roll along it all in good time.

There is no point in pushing for the future next, for it is in conception and not ready for birth.

Everything is perfect and you are doing perfectly well.

We can't find the solution when we are staring at the problem, rather distract from the problem and the solution will offer itself.

There are days when nothing will shift the feeling in the house and everything seems chaotic.

Babies cry and we can't find the reason, children have squabbles and the dog is always under foot.

Sometimes we can get so serious about finding the reason we go around in circles and there's a simpler solution to shifting gears.

Grab everyone and get out of the house!

When we remove ourselves and our families from an atmosphere and get out,

even for a short period of time,

it's like a giant reset button on the day and we find that when we re-enter the house,

it's never the same as how we left it.

A child at any age can experience fear.

Fear is an indicator of lack of connection for none of us can be connected to our source of love and feel afraid.

Therefore, whereas we often want to hunt out the cause of the fear, (such as a scary movie, book, or incident) and get rid of it, all the cause did was disconnect our children from who they really are.

If we focus too much on the fear, we can create more of the feeling of it.

A clearer route to helping our children through their fear is to find that connection point again.

To play with them, love them, make them laugh, make them feel secure in everything they are and in the love and wellbeing that surrounds them.

For where the feeling of love is,

fear cannot exist.

A conscious parent is a listening parent.

Yes, sometimes it is actually harder than we think it should be.

Sometimes, especially when you have more than one child in your life, it seems like everything happens at once.

It's not that we don't listen to our children, it's that we're only half listening to everyone and only half conscious of everything else.

Phones ring, toast burns and thoughts chatter.

However, when we take some time out just to be with our children,

when we sit on the floor and play,

when we ask about their day and listen to their problems, even if we just ask them to read to us out loud, when we hear, process and feel what our children say we open a window and set them free, validating them to be who they really are without trying to get our attention some other way.

Remember that feeling when you were little and someone walked in when you were playing an imaginary game?

Do you ever feel the same sense of self-consciousness when playing with your children?

What a thing to be able to overcome now. What a thing for our children to offer us.

Each day our children welcome us to play, sing, dance, act silly, laugh and have fun with them,

if we only get over the idea of looking like we're grown up.

No one is watching and it is a far greater gift to offer our children the perspective that we all come to this world to experience the fun and adventure of it all,

rather than constantly remind them

that one day the fun ends and we all have to grow up.

We must remember that our children, as well as ourselves, are changeable.

Their likes, preferences, opinions, and desires will shift and change as they grow and if we use these as ways to define them to ourselves, we'll get left behind in the shuffle.

We all know what it's like to be seen as the same person we were years ago.

We all have been told how much we like some music or color, when we changed our minds years ago.

We've all been judged by our past and felt it didn't belong to us.

We have to allow our children to change their minds.

The only way we can really know them, is to rely and focus on their true essence and who they really are,

enjoying them as they journey through life exploring all it has to offer.

There will always be days where everything seems to go completely haywire and the more we try to get things "under control" the crazier they become.

It will always be the same, when we focus on how crazy it is, we call more chaos forth.

It is in the hectic moments when it is the most important to call attention to the things that go well.

When we stop mid-chaos and look at something that brings us relief,

from our children, our spouse, our pets, our flowers, even the blue sky or our favorite song,

we relax and that become the new feeling space of the day.

Things will start to match the new feeling state and we will start to appreciate even those things that created chaos moments before.

The Addiction to Friction is what keeps us in that state.

Friction, or chaos happens to everyone, it's our focus on it that perpetuates more.

Often Who We Are is overshadowed by Who We Want to Be.

Yes, it is good to have high ideals; yes it is great to have vision.

However, with those aspirations we can often put ourselves in a place where we feel bad if we don't match our dream version of ourselves.

We feel guilty if we get frustrated or disappointed if we sigh with relief when bedtime comes, simply because in our ideal version of us, we wouldn't do that.

We block inspired solutions, because we're focused on our disillusionment.

When we decide to be happy with Who We Are, we can see the frustration, and offer it up for solutions to do better tomorrow.

When we put attention on being Who We Are we allow everything we've become to this point take effect and not muddy the water by trying to be too much all at once.

Tomorrow may see us differently. We are all progressing forward, all expanding and changing.

Our children have their own things going off in their minds, and sometimes how things unfold within a day totally baffles them rather than progresses in the way it makes sense to us.

When a child melts down

and everything seems to be a big deal,

it is often because it is.

It's a big deal to live a life you don't fully understand.

Therefore, no matter how often we discuss things with our partners, our parents and our friends, our children need to hear it all as well, to know what's going off in their worlds and how all the pieces fit together.

It's their story too, and sometimes they need to hear it to fully comprehend it.

Otherwise it's just walking in shadows.

When a child is fussy or acting unlike themselves then often the simple act of playing with them can call them back to themselves.

It's so easy to fall back into the habit of saying no or getting stressed and upset, when really they are trying to stop life from being confusing and slow it down so they can get connected.

When we ourselves get connected we can feel our way to what our children are crying out for, and often,

unless they are sick or tired,

a focused game of some sort will call them back.

Play can connect us as well,

so it's a double bonus!

Even in being a Spiritually Aware Parent it is easy to slip into the Should rant.

"I should feel happier." "My children should be more focused", "My day should be calmer", "My children should get along." "I should appreciate more." "I should meditate more."

From those shoulds, the next step is judgment and it's impossible to feel better when we judge and criticize either ourselves or others.

Therefore, whenever one of those shoulds rise up within us, we can shift it from a feeling of failure to a feeling of new desire. We can offer it up as something we want and stay open to it becoming part of the New Now, without feeling guilt over it not being in our present moment.

We are on a journey with our children. Even if they never had something you feel "should" have been there before, it means that now is an even better time to try it.

Trust the journey, and have faith that our children are getting exactly what they need.

There is always indicators present in our day to day that tell us how connected we are or how not.

There is no such thing as a run of bad luck, rather when things continually go wrong, it is best to take a step back and start to let go of the little things that challenge us from feeling good.

When we let go of those little things we resent without even noticing, or worry about but tell ourselves we don't, then suddenly we attract differently.

We avoid parking tickets even though we missed spotting the fire hydrant; we catch a child falling, and find the change in the sofa that we just needed.

When we clean up those little things that throw us off, suddenly we appear to have the golden touch.

When we let go of those things we hold on to, and then shift onto appreciating the things we have, then life rolls merrily along.

*All is well. All is well. All is well, all the time,
even if we get hurt, we make mistakes, and
things go wrong.*

*But often when it passes, when all is right
again, we look back and we know that it was
right that the wrong happened.*

*Often, we know we have expanded and
grown for it,*

*that it has pushed us to a greater, maybe
wiser, NOW.*

All is well.

*Often when we are upset we can set ourselves
apart from our tears and witness our own
sadness.*

*From that position we can also sense the
stream of well being, of love, flowing around
us.*

*All is well. We may not feel it all the time,
but still Love and Well being keeps flowing
endlessly*

*and it makes all the difference to trust in its
powers of transformation.*

We are tool providers.

Sometimes when our children are feeling especially off, sometimes falling into traps of self pity, resentment or anger simply by the thought processes that have become the habit to them, we have to rise to the occasion and offer tools to shift perspective.

Yes, it is vital to support our children in how they feel. Yes, it is important for them to feel comfortable to express those feelings.

However, if the same negative emotion is being expressed over and over, then the perspective has become habitual and it is our time to step in and help re-direct if we can.

It helps to teach a child about the Law of Attraction, for how we feel at our default level is what is matched by universal powers. It also helps to offer tools to look for alternate perspectives, to ask questions like "find 5 things that are going well in life."

We are tool providers and one of those tools is to help our children build awareness to how they feel, and who they are. It's not to stand by and comfort someone each time they go down the spiral of feeling off.

That simply confirms the offness.

Fear is always an option for a parent.

We can be fearful of our children's future, worry how they will "turn out", be scared that they'll get mixed up with something they'll regret, concerned they'll lose their lunch money!

When we let the fear beast get hold of us, there's an endless list of what we can worry about.

But when we take a step back and remind ourselves that we are on a journey and so are they,

that our lives are a constant stream of circumstances that offer us opportunity to be who we want to be, and we follow our inner source to speak to them,

then we can look at our children and tell them that as long as they follow their heart and feel fully like themselves,

than they are doing exceptionally well.

Within the space of connection is where everything lies.

When something troubles you: go within. When you are stressed: go within.

When you don't know what to do: go within.

When you can't figure out what your child needs: go within.

Whenever you find a spare moment, go within and connect with everything you truly are.

Trust who you are.

Trust that your children choose you.

Trust that inner voice.

Be You at your fullest and within that be the parent you dream you can be.

Children sense our fear and our own sense of drama and if we seem distracted and distant from them at these times it can leave them feeling overwhelmed.

However, often emergencies can prove to be fond memories for young children when they grow older as there is a sense of a family bonding together, spending time together in the dark, being inventive together and basically being in each other's focus without the usual day to day runaround which has had to be stopped in its tracks.

In any out of the ordinary situation,

be safe and then take moments to "be" with your children,

cuddle and tell stories and create an atmosphere of love, warmth and security.

Be well, happy and thrive and create memories of adventure and family unity within your home.

Negative thoughts will always flow in.

Sometimes they will be ones that can easily be shifted and a better feeling version can be found quickly.

However, there are other negative thoughts that are more concrete, that when we think them, and feel them, they perpetuate a series of like thoughts and we can feel a spiral begin.

I like to call these a "nail in the coffin" thought, as they start to form how we feel and taint our reactions to everything.

When we feel ourselves think a negative thought and in turn feel the negative emotion linked to it, if we ask ourselves whether it's just a negative thought floating through or if it's a "nail in the coffin" thought, then we can deal with it instantaneously,

seeing the drama behind them, seeing the process they lead to,

and steering our ships clear of stormy weather.

What children understand,

and what we are so easy to forget,

is that life is about living.

No matter how much we crave for the more,
for the knowledge,

the explanation,

the reason,

the understanding,

in fact what we are here to do is to Live life
to its fullest and to have fun.

The tools that we find in our search for
understanding are usually for the benefit of
living life even better.

The better we live the better we feel,

the better we feel the better we live.

Laugh, live and breathe.

All is truly as it should be.

For more information regarding
Spiritually Aware Parenting
and the work of Christina Fletcher,
please visit her website:
www.spirituallyawareparenting.com
or the Spiritually Aware Parenting
Facebook page
www.facebook.com/whotheyreallyare